How to Create a Su YouTube Channel

Introduction:

Welcome to the comprehensive guide on crafting a triumphant YouTube channel that captivates audiences and drives your online presence to new heights. In this Ebook, we delve into the art and science of building a prosperous YouTube channel from scratch. Whether you're an aspiring content creator or a seasoned vlogger aiming to refine your strategy, this resource is your compass to success.

Embark on a journey where creativity meets strategy, and discover the core principles that underpin a thriving YouTube venture. From honing your content niche to mastering the art of video production, we'll navigate through every step with meticulous detail. Uncover the secrets of enhancing engagement, expanding your subscriber base, and fostering a community that resonates with your unique voice.

Drawing from the experiences of accomplished YouTubers and industry experts, this guide equips you with actionable insights and practical tips that cater to the dynamic landscape of online video. Our mission is to empower you to overcome challenges, leverage algorithmic trends, and unleash your channel's full potential.

Whether you aspire to educate, entertain, or inspire, this Ebook is your blueprint to creating a YouTube channel that not only flourishes but leaves an indelible mark on the digital realm. Join us as we unlock the doors to YouTube success, one chapter at a time.

Certainly, here are 15 ways to create a successful YouTube channel:

1. Niche Expertise: Determine your niche and become an authority in that area. Focusing on a specific topic helps attract a dedicated audience.
2. Compelling Content: Craft high-quality, engaging content that captivates viewers and keeps them coming back for more.

3. Consistent Schedule: Establish a consistent upload schedule to build anticipation and maintain viewer loyalty.
4. SEO Mastery: Understand and implement effective search engine optimization (SEO) techniques to make your videos discoverable.
5. Eye-Catching Thumbnails: Design visually appealing thumbnails that entice viewers to click on your videos.
6. Engaging Titles: Create attention-grabbing titles that accurately represent your content and spark curiosity.
7. Audience Interaction: Foster a sense of community by responding to comments, asking for feedback, and incorporating viewer suggestions.
8. Social Media Promotion: Utilize various social media platforms to promote your videos and engage with a wider audience.
9. Collaborations: Collaborate with fellow YouTubers to cross-promote and tap into their audiences.
10. Analytics Insight: Regularly analyze your video performance using analytics tools to refine your strategy based on viewer trends.
11. Mobile-Friendly Content: Ensure your videos are optimized for mobile viewing, as a significant portion of YouTube traffic comes from mobile devices.
12. Compelling Introductions: Hook viewers from the start with engaging introductions that highlight the value of your content.
13. Storyboarding: Plan your videos with clear storyboards to maintain a coherent structure and narrative flow.
14. Personal Branding: Develop a strong and relatable personal brand that resonates with your target audience.
15. Patience and Persistence: Building a successful YouTube channel takes time. Stay patient, adapt to changes, and persistently refine your approach.

By incorporating these 15 strategies into your YouTube journey, you'll be well on your way to creating a channel that stands out, engages viewers, and achieves lasting success.

1 **Niche Expertise: Determine your niche and become an authority in that area. Focusing on a specific topic helps attract a dedicated audience.**

Crafting Compelling Content: The Art of Captivating and Retaining YouTube Viewers

In the ever-evolving digital landscape, the art of creating compelling content stands as the cornerstone of building a successful YouTube channel that not only captures attention but also fosters a loyal and engaged audience. This pivotal strategy centres on the creation of high-quality, engaging videos that resonate deeply with viewers, encouraging them to not only consume your content but also eagerly anticipate its next iteration. By mastering the craft of content creation, you unlock the potential to establish a lasting presence in the vast and competitive realm of online video.

Unravelling the Essence of Compelling Content

Compelling content transcends mere information dissemination; it weaves a narrative that resonates with viewers on an emotional level. Such content possesses the power to evoke curiosity, elicit laughter, spark introspection, or provide solutions to real-world challenges. It marries substance with style, delivering value while capturing the viewer's imagination. Through compelling content, you create an immersive experience that goes beyond the screen, leaving an indelible mark on the viewer's memory.

The Engaging Equation: Quality and Relevance

Quality and relevance are twin pillars that underpin compelling content. Quality encompasses the technical aspects of production, including video resolution, audio clarity, and visual aesthetics. Investing time in improving these elements elevates the viewer's experience and reflects your commitment to delivering excellence. Additionally, relevance is paramount. Your content must address the interests, concerns, and aspirations of your target audience. Understanding your viewers' needs ensures that each video serves a purpose, increasing the likelihood of engagement and sharing.

Cracking the Engagement Code: Storytelling and Connection

Storytelling forms the beating heart of engaging content. Through narratives, anecdotes, or relatable experiences, you transport viewers into your world, making them emotionally invested in your content. A compelling story holds the power to transcend mere information and form a deep connection with the audience. Share personal insights, struggles, or triumphs, as this vulnerability humanises your content and resonates with viewers on a personal level.

The Golden Rule: Audience-Centric Approach

Creating content that captivates and retains viewers necessitates an audience-centric approach. It's imperative to have a crystal-clear understanding of your target demographic – their preferences, interests, and pain points. Tailor your content to cater to their desires and offer solutions to their challenges. Engage with your audience through comments, surveys, and social media interactions to gain insights that refine your content strategy and foster a sense of community.

Variety and Consistency: A Delicate Balance

While diversity in content is essential to maintain viewer interest, consistency is equally crucial. Establishing a consistent posting schedule instils a sense of anticipation among your audience, ensuring they return eagerly for your new releases. Balance variety with consistency by experimenting with different formats, such as tutorials, vlogs, challenges, or behind-the-scenes glimpses. This diversity keeps your content fresh while staying true to your channel's identity.

Analytics: The Guiding Light of Improvement

In the digital realm, analytics are your compass to navigating content creation. Regularly analyse video performance metrics, such as watch time, audience retention, and click-through rates. These insights illuminate what works and what requires refinement. Embrace a willingness to adapt based on data-driven feedback, leading to continuous improvement and a better understanding of your audience's preferences.

Harnessing Technology: Visual Appeal and Innovation

Technology is a potent ally in the creation of compelling content. Leverage editing tools to enhance visual appeal, adding dynamic graphics, transitions, and effects that elevate the viewing experience. Embrace emerging technologies, such as virtual reality or interactive elements, to push creative boundaries and engage viewers in innovative ways.

The Journey of Value: Education, Entertainment, Inspiration

Compelling content takes on various forms, each offering distinct value to the viewer. Educational content imparts knowledge, insights, or tutorials that empower viewers with new skills. Entertainment content aims to amuse, evoke laughter, or immerse viewers in captivating narratives. Inspirational content motivates and resonates on an emotional level, encouraging viewers to reflect and take action. A balanced combination of these elements caters to diverse viewer preferences.

The Legacy of Compelling Content: Lasting Impact

In conclusion, the creation of compelling content embodies an artful fusion of quality, relevance, storytelling, and audience connection. By mastering this craft, you forge an enduring connection with your audience, establishing a channel that not only captures their attention but also leaves an indelible imprint on their lives. Through each video, you contribute to a legacy of engagement, growth, and community. As you embark on the journey of content creation, remember that the magic lies in your ability to craft content that not only captivates for a moment but lingers in the minds and hearts of viewers long after the screen fades to black.

2 Compelling Content: Craft high-quality, engaging content that captivates viewers and keeps them coming back for more.

Crafting Compelling Content: The Art of Captivating and Retaining YouTube Viewers

In the ever-evolving digital landscape, the art of creating compelling content stands as the cornerstone of building a successful YouTube channel that not only captures attention but also fosters a loyal and engaged audience. This pivotal strategy centres on the creation of high-quality, engaging videos that resonate deeply with viewers, encouraging them to not only consume your content but also eagerly anticipate its next iteration. By mastering the craft of content creation, you unlock the potential to establish a lasting presence in the vast and competitive realm of online video.

Unravelling the Essence of Compelling Content

Compelling content transcends mere information dissemination; it weaves a narrative that resonates with viewers on an emotional level. Such content possesses the power to evoke curiosity, elicit laughter, spark introspection, or provide solutions to real-world challenges. It marries substance with style, delivering value while capturing the viewer's imagination. Through compelling content, you create an immersive experience that goes beyond the screen, leaving an indelible mark on the viewer's memory.

The Engaging Equation: Quality and Relevance

Quality and relevance are twin pillars that underpin compelling content. Quality encompasses the technical aspects of production, including video resolution, audio clarity, and visual aesthetics. Investing time in improving these elements elevates the viewer's experience and reflects your commitment to delivering excellence. Additionally, relevance is paramount. Your content must address the interests, concerns, and aspirations of your target audience. Understanding your viewers' needs ensures that each video serves a purpose, increasing the likelihood of engagement and sharing.

Cracking the Engagement Code: Storytelling and Connection

Storytelling forms the beating heart of engaging content. Through narratives, anecdotes, or relatable experiences, you transport viewers into your world, making them emotionally invested in your content. A compelling story holds the power to transcend mere information and form a deep connection with the audience. Share personal insights, struggles, or triumphs, as this vulnerability humanises your content and resonates with viewers on a personal level.

The Golden Rule: Audience-Centric Approach

Creating content that captivates and retains viewers necessitates an audience-centric approach. It's imperative to have a crystal-clear understanding of your target demographic – their preferences, interests, and pain points. Tailor your content to cater to their desires and offer solutions to their challenges. Engage with your audience through comments, surveys, and social media interactions to gain insights that refine your content strategy and foster a sense of community.

Variety and Consistency: A Delicate Balance

While diversity in content is essential to maintain viewer interest, consistency is equally crucial. Establishing a consistent posting schedule instils a sense of anticipation among your audience, ensuring they return eagerly for your new releases. Balance variety with consistency by experimenting with different formats, such as tutorials, vlogs, challenges, or behind-the-scenes glimpses. This diversity keeps your content fresh while staying true to your channel's identity.

Analytics: The Guiding Light of Improvement

In the digital realm, analytics are your compass to navigating content creation. Regularly analyse video performance metrics, such as watch time, audience retention, and click-through rates. These insights illuminate what works and what requires refinement. Embrace a willingness to adapt based on data-driven feedback, leading to continuous improvement and a better understanding of your audience's preferences.

Harnessing Technology: Visual Appeal and Innovation

Technology is a potent ally in the creation of compelling content. Leverage editing tools to enhance visual appeal, adding dynamic graphics, transitions, and effects that elevate the viewing experience. Embrace emerging technologies, such as virtual reality or interactive elements, to push creative boundaries and engage viewers in innovative ways.

The Journey of Value: Education, Entertainment, Inspiration

Compelling content takes on various forms, each offering distinct value to the viewer. Educational content imparts knowledge, insights, or tutorials that empower viewers with new skills. Entertainment content aims to amuse, evoke laughter, or immerse viewers in captivating narratives. Inspirational content motivates and resonates on an emotional level, encouraging viewers to reflect and take action. A balanced combination of these elements caters to diverse viewer preferences.

The Legacy of Compelling Content: Lasting Impact

In conclusion, the creation of compelling content embodies an artful fusion of quality, relevance, storytelling, and audience connection. By mastering this craft, you forge an enduring connection with your audience, establishing a channel that not only captures their attention but also leaves an indelible imprint on their lives. Through each video, you contribute to a legacy of engagement, growth, and community. As you embark on the journey of content creation, remember that the magic lies in your ability to craft content that not only captivates for a moment but lingers in the minds and hearts of viewers long after the screen fades to black.

3 Consistent Schedule: Establish a consistent upload schedule to build anticipation and maintain viewer loyalty.

Building Anticipation and Fostering Loyalty: The Significance of a Consistent YouTube Upload Schedule

In the bustling universe of YouTube content creation, the establishment of a consistent upload schedule stands as a cornerstone strategy to not only nurture viewer loyalty but also to cultivate a sense of anticipation that propels your channel towards success. This deliberate approach entails committing to a predictable rhythm of video releases, a practice that not only enhances viewer engagement but also fosters a dedicated audience who eagerly await your content. By weaving the tapestry of a consistent schedule, you unlock the potential to form lasting connections and amplify the impact of your online presence.

Unveiling the Essence of Consistency

Consistency on YouTube is akin to the rhythm of a heartbeat – it signifies stability, reliability, and a deliberate commitment to delivering value to your audience. A consistent upload schedule goes beyond the mere act of posting videos; it embodies your dedication to your craft and your respect for your viewers' time. It forms a pact of trust between you and your audience, assuring them that they can count on fresh content at predictable intervals.

The Magnetic Pull of Anticipation

Consistency in your upload schedule instils a sense of anticipation within your audience. Human psychology is wired to seek patterns and predictability, and when viewers know when to expect new content from you, they eagerly await its arrival. This anticipation elevates the viewing experience – each video becomes an event, a moment to look forward to. This sense of excitement becomes a driving force that keeps your audience engaged and invested in your content journey.

Viewer Loyalty: The Cornerstone of Success

Viewer loyalty is the bedrock on which successful YouTube channels are built. A consistent upload schedule plays a pivotal role in nurturing this loyalty. When viewers know that your content reliably arrives at specific times, they are more likely to subscribe, engage, and actively participate in your channel's community. This loyalty extends beyond the screen – it's the bond you cultivate with your audience that compels them to share your content, offer feedback, and even defend your channel amidst the sea of online distractions.

Creating a Habitual Viewing Experience

Consistency breeds habit. Over time, your audience becomes accustomed to your schedule, and watching your videos becomes a part of their routine. Just as people tune in to their favorite TV shows at specific times, your viewers will align their schedules with your content releases. This habitual viewing experience bolsters your channel's presence in their lives and makes it a familiar and comforting aspect of their online journey.

Balancing Quantity and Quality

While a consistent upload schedule is vital, it's equally important to strike a balance between quantity and quality. Consistency should never compromise the quality of your content. Each video should meet the high standards you've set for your channel. If adhering to a daily upload schedule impacts the quality of your content, consider a more manageable frequency that allows you to deliver excellence without burnout.

The Mechanism of Planning

A consistent upload schedule requires careful planning. Begin by determining the frequency of your uploads – whether it's weekly, bi-weekly, or monthly. Factor in your content creation process, allowing ample time for research, scripting, filming, editing, and any other necessary tasks. Create a content calendar that outlines release dates and topics, giving you a roadmap to follow and ensuring that your schedule remains steady.

Open Communication and Flexibility

While consistency is crucial, life is often unpredictable. Sometimes, unforeseen circumstances might disrupt your upload schedule. In such cases, communication is key. If you're unable to release a video as planned, communicate with your audience through social media or a quick update video. Transparency about any changes helps maintain trust and keeps your audience informed.

Evolving with Your Audience

As your channel grows, your audience's preferences and habits might evolve. Stay attuned to feedback and analytics, and be willing to adapt your upload schedule if necessary. Flexibility is essential to align with your audience's changing needs while maintaining the core principle of consistent content delivery.

The Legacy of Consistency: Lasting Impact

In conclusion, a consistent YouTube upload schedule is a dynamic force that underpins audience loyalty and builds anticipation. It's the vehicle through which you shape your channel's identity, weave connections, and contribute to the narrative of your viewers' lives. The consistency you infuse into your content creation journey transcends the digital realm, becoming an enduring legacy of trust, engagement, and community. As you embark on this path, remember that the rhythm you establish resonates not just in the frequency of your video releases, but in the hearts of those who eagerly await each upload.

4 SEO Mastery: Understand and implement effective search engine optimization (SEO) techniques to make your videos discoverable.

Unlocking Visibility: The Art of SEO Mastery for Discoverable YouTube Videos

In the bustling universe of YouTube, the mastery of Search Engine Optimization (SEO) stands as a critical cornerstone for creators seeking to amplify their video's discoverability and reach a wider audience. This strategic practice involves understanding and implementing techniques that optimize your content for search engines, making your videos more likely to surface in relevant searches. By harnessing the power of SEO, you not only enhance your video's visibility but also position your channel as a valuable resource in the vast landscape of online content.

Decoding the Essence of SEO

At its core, SEO is about aligning your content with the intent of online users. It involves understanding the keywords, phrases, and topics that your target audience is likely to search for. By integrating these terms organically into your video titles, descriptions, and tags, you increase the likelihood of your videos appearing in search results. SEO transforms your content from a needle in the haystack to a beacon that guides interested viewers to your videos.

The Power of Discovery: Appearing in Search Results

SEO is akin to placing your content on a well-travelled path. When users type in keywords related to your video's topic, effective SEO ensures that your content is among the top search results. This visibility translates into increased views, engagement, and the potential to attract new subscribers. With millions of videos vying for attention, SEO becomes your compass, directing viewers towards your content amidst the digital noise.

The Keyword Ecosystem: Research and Application

Keyword research is the foundation of effective SEO. Start by identifying the primary keywords that are relevant to your video's topic. Utilize keyword research tools to gauge search volumes and competition. Incorporate a mix of high-volume and long-tail keywords that accurately represent your content. However, avoid keyword stuffing – the seamless integration of keywords into your metadata is crucial for both user experience and search engine algorithms.

Title Tag Mastery: The Gateway to Clicks

The title tag is your video's first impression. Craft titles that are not only descriptive but also engaging. Incorporate your primary keyword near the beginning of the title to immediately signal its relevance to search engines. An appealing title compels users to click and explore further, driving up your video's click-through rate (CTR), which is a positive signal for search algorithms.

Descriptions: Informative and Engaging

Your video's description is an opportunity to provide additional context and information. Incorporate relevant keywords naturally within the description while maintaining a conversational tone. A comprehensive description offers viewers an overview of the video's content, encouraging them to watch. Additionally, include relevant links to your other videos, playlists, or external resources, enhancing the viewer's engagement and journey within your content ecosystem.

Tags: Bridging the Gap Between Content and Search

Tags serve as bridges that connect your video's content with user queries. Include a mix of broad and specific tags that encompass your video's core topics. Incorporate variations of your keywords and consider tags related to trending or related subjects. While tags play a crucial role in SEO, their influence has diminished over time, but they still contribute to your video's overall discoverability.

Thumbnail and Video Transcript: SEO Beyond Text

While SEO largely revolves around textual elements, non-textual aspects also play a role. Thumbnails are visual cues that entice users to click on your video. Ensure that your thumbnail aligns with your video's content and is visually appealing. Additionally, providing accurate video transcripts enhances accessibility and can indirectly contribute to SEO by making your content more comprehensible for search engine crawlers.

Engagement Metrics: The SEO Boosters

Engagement metrics, such as watch time and likes, signal to search engines that your content is valuable and relevant. High engagement rates indicate viewer satisfaction, which in turn influences your video's ranking in search results. Crafting high-quality, engaging content that keeps viewers watching and encourages interaction directly impacts your SEO efforts.

Adapting to Algorithmic Changes

Search engine algorithms evolve to provide users with the best possible experience. As a creator, staying informed about algorithmic updates is crucial. Adapt your SEO strategies to align with these changes while maintaining your focus on producing valuable, relevant content. Continuous learning and agility in your approach ensure that your content remains discoverable amidst shifting digital landscapes.

The Journey of Discovery: A Legacy of Impact

In conclusion, SEO mastery is an indispensable tool in a creator's arsenal, guiding their content towards the eyes of interested viewers. By understanding and implementing effective SEO techniques, you navigate the labyrinthine pathways of search engines, leading viewers to your videos. Your journey involves meticulous research, strategic implementation, and an unwavering commitment to delivering value. The legacy of SEO extends beyond the technical realm – it's the impact you leave on viewers who discover and engage with your content, and the lasting connection you forge in the realm of online exploration. As you delve into the world of SEO, remember that every optimised element contributes to a symphony that resonates in the hearts and screens of those who seek knowledge, entertainment, and inspiration.

5 Eye-Catching Thumbnails: Design visually appealing thumbnails that entice viewers to click on your videos.

The Art of Visual Seduction: Crafting Compelling Thumbnails to Capture Viewer Attention

In the dynamic realm of YouTube content creation, the mastery of eye-catching thumbnails stands as a pivotal strategy for creators seeking to entice viewers and elevate their video's click-through rates. These miniature visual representations encapsulate the essence of your content, serving as the first point of contact between your video and potential viewers. By wielding the power of captivating thumbnails, you not only enhance your video's discoverability but also draw audiences into your narrative, fostering engagement and ultimately boosting the success of your channel.

Unveiling the Essence of Thumbnails

Thumbnails are digital storefronts, windows into the world you've meticulously crafted within your video. These compact images function as visual teasers, offering a sneak peek into the content's value and relevance. A well-crafted thumbnail is a beacon that beckons viewers to venture further, a first impression that holds the potential to determine whether a video is clicked on or overlooked.

The Intrigue of First Impressions

In the realm of digital content, first impressions are irreplaceable. Thumbnails serve as this initial point of contact, exerting a powerful influence on a viewer's decision to engage. An eye-catching thumbnail is the virtual equivalent of locking eyes with someone across a room – it sparks curiosity, triggers an emotional connection, and invites further exploration. In a sea of content thumbnails, yours must be the one that triggers that spark of intrigue.

Design Principles: The Art of Compelling Imagery

Crafting an effective thumbnail requires an artistic blend of design principles and a deep understanding of your content's essence. A compelling thumbnail encapsulates the video's main message, often through a high-resolution image or a carefully selected frame. Leveraging bold typography, vibrant colours, and

13

visually striking elements can create contrast and make your thumbnail pop against the backdrop of search results or suggested videos.

Captivating Emotion: Eliciting Curiosity and Desire

Emotion is the currency of visual communication. A thumbnail should evoke emotion, whether it's curiosity, amusement, empathy, or excitement. Choosing an image that encapsulates the most intriguing aspect of your video's content and aligns with the emotional journey you wish to take your viewers on can be a powerful strategy. It's the promise of an emotional payoff that compels users to click and explore.

Alignment with Content: The Promise Fulfilled

An effective thumbnail does more than just capture attention – it sets expectations for the content within. Ensure that your thumbnail accurately represents the essence of your video. Misleading thumbnails can lead to high click-through rates but low viewer retention, damaging your channel's credibility and reputation. Honesty in thumbnail representation builds trust with your audience, encouraging longer watch times and fostering repeat viewership.

The Power of Contrast and Simplicity

Human eyes are naturally drawn to contrast and simplicity. Incorporate elements that stand out against the thumbnail's background, whether it's a bold colour, a striking image, or clear typography. Avoid clutter and ensure that your thumbnail's message is conveyed with simplicity and clarity. This approach facilitates swift comprehension and aids viewers in making an informed decision about engaging with your content.

Typography: Words That Spark Interest

Typography within thumbnails acts as a supplementary means of communication. Use concise, attention-grabbing text that complements the visual elements. Craft a compelling title or incorporate keywords that reinforce the content's value proposition. The typography's style, size, and colour should align with your channel's branding while remaining legible across devices and screen sizes.

Testing and Refinement: Iterative Excellence

The art of thumbnail creation is a dynamic process that thrives on testing and refinement. Analyze the performance of your thumbnails using analytics tools, paying attention to click-through rates and viewer engagement. Experiment with variations of imagery, text, and design elements to identify what resonates most effectively with your audience. This iterative approach ensures that your thumbnails continually evolve to capture maximum attention.

Branding: Consistency in Visual Identity

As your channel grows, your thumbnails become a recognisable hallmark of your brand. Consistency in your thumbnail design – from colour schemes to typography – cultivates a visual identity that sets your content apart. When viewers associate your thumbnails with quality, relevance, and entertainment, they are more likely to click, watch, and share.

Impact Beyond the Click: Crafting a Lasting Connection

In conclusion, crafting compelling thumbnails is an art that transcends mere visuals – it's a language of seduction that lures viewers into the realm of your content. By mastering the principles of design, emotion, and alignment, you create thumbnails that not only capture clicks but forge a lasting connection with your audience. Your thumbnail is the gateway to your content's narrative, a promise of value that beckons viewers to embark on a journey of discovery. As you hone your thumbnail crafting skills, remember that behind each captivating image lies the potential to captivate minds, hearts, and screens, leaving an indelible mark in the vibrant universe of YouTube.

6 Engaging Titles: Create attention-grabbing titles that accurately represent your content and spark curiosity.

The Art of Enticing Exploration: Crafting Engaging Titles to Ignite Curiosity and Reflect Content

In the dynamic realm of YouTube content creation, the mastery of engaging titles stands as a pivotal strategy for creators seeking to captivate viewers' attention and lure them into the immersive experience of their videos. These succinct strings of words serve as digital invitations, encapsulating the essence of your content while sparking curiosity and anticipation. By wielding the power of engaging titles, you not only enhance your video's discoverability but also entice audiences to delve deeper into your narrative, fostering engagement and ultimately elevating the success of your channel.

Unveiling the Essence of Engaging Titles

Engaging titles are not mere labels; they are the embodiment of your content's promise. These carefully crafted phrases are the first touchpoint between your video and potential viewers. An engaging title has the potency to evoke emotion, resonate with a viewer's interests, and compel them to take the next step – clicking to explore your video further.

Curiosity: The Catalyst of Engagement

Curiosity is the driving force behind human exploration, and engaging titles are its catalysts. Crafting a title that piques curiosity primes viewers for an intriguing experience. The title acts as a teaser, hinting at the adventure that awaits within your video. Whether it's through posing a question, teasing a surprising revelation, or presenting a captivating concept, your title should create a mental itch that viewers can't resist scratching.

Reflecting Content: The Promise Fulfilled

While sparking curiosity is vital, an engaging title must also accurately represent your video's content. The title is a promise you make to your audience – it sets expectations that your video must deliver upon. Misleading titles can lead to viewer dissatisfaction, hampering your channel's credibility and trustworthiness. An authentic title ensures that viewers find what they expect, building trust and encouraging repeat viewership.

The Balance of Brevity and Descriptiveness

Engaging titles exist at the intersection of brevity and descriptiveness. While it's important to capture attention in a concise manner, your title should also provide enough context to convey what your video is about. Consider including keywords that highlight the main topic while maintaining an element of intrigue. Striking this balance ensures that your title is both informative and alluring.

Emotionally Charged Language: Invoking Feeling

Language is a conduit for emotion, and engaging titles leverage this power. Incorporating emotionally charged words can evoke a visceral response in viewers. Depending on your content's tone, you might use words that evoke curiosity, excitement, surprise, or empathy. This emotional resonance forms a connection with your audience before they even click on your video.

Keyword Integration: Aligning with Search Intent

Effective titles seamlessly integrate relevant keywords that align with users' search intent. Conduct keyword research to identify the phrases that your target audience is likely to search for. Incorporate these keywords into your title while maintaining natural language flow. This integration not only enhances your video's search engine visibility but also signals its relevance to potential viewers.

A/B Testing: Iterative Refinement

Crafting engaging titles is an iterative process that benefits from experimentation and refinement. Consider A/B testing different title variations to gauge their performance. Analyze metrics such as click-through rates and viewer retention to identify which titles resonate most effectively with your audience. This data-driven approach empowers you to continually improve your title crafting skills.

The Power of the First Impression

In a world of fleeting attention spans, the first impression is a potent currency. Engaging titles provide your video with that essential initial impact. Just as a captivating headline in a newspaper compels you to read an article, a well-crafted title compels viewers to click and engage. This click is the first step in the journey of viewer interaction, making the title a pivotal gateway to your content's narrative.

Branding: Consistency and Identity

As your channel grows, your titles become an integral part of your brand's identity. Consistency in your title style, tone, and formatting cultivates recognisability. Viewers who consistently encounter engaging titles associated with quality content are more likely to click, watch, and become subscribers. This alignment builds your channel's reputation as a source of valuable and captivating content.

Impact Beyond the Click: A Journey of Engagement

In conclusion, the creation of engaging titles is an artful blend of curiosity, authenticity, and relevance. By mastering the principles of language, emotion, and search intent, you craft titles that not only capture clicks but also set the stage for a meaningful interaction between your content and your audience. Your titles are the trailheads of exploration, beckoning viewers to embark on a journey that holds the promise of discovery. As you refine your title crafting skills, remember that each thoughtfully chosen word holds the potential to ignite curiosity, forge connections, and leave a lasting imprint in the vibrant realm of YouTube.

7 Audience Interaction: Foster a sense of community by responding to comments, asking for feedback, and incorporating viewer suggestions.

Forging Bonds Beyond the Screen: Nurturing Audience Interaction for a Vibrant YouTube Community

In the ever-evolving landscape of YouTube content creation, the art of fostering audience interaction stands as a pivotal strategy for creators aiming to transcend the screen and cultivate a thriving community. This deliberate practice involves engaging with viewers through comments, inviting feedback, and incorporating their suggestions into your content. By weaving the threads of audience interaction, you not only amplify viewer engagement but also create a sense of belonging that transforms passive viewers into active participants and loyal advocates of your channel.

Unveiling the Essence of Audience Interaction

Audience interaction is the bridge that connects the creator with their viewers. It's a testament to the two-way nature of the digital medium, transforming what was once a one-sided communication into a dynamic conversation. By acknowledging, responding to, and incorporating viewer input, creators create a powerful feedback loop that informs content decisions, enhances engagement, and fosters a sense of community.

The Power of Connection: Personalized Engagement

Audience interaction is more than a mere checkbox; it's an opportunity to establish a personal connection with your viewers. Responding to comments not only acknowledges your audience's presence but also validates their engagement. This personalized touch demonstrates that you value their time and opinions, cultivating a connection that goes beyond the video itself.

Feedback as a Growth Catalyst

Feedback is the lifeblood of improvement. By inviting viewers to share their thoughts, creators open doors to invaluable insights. Constructive criticism and positive affirmations alike provide

18

perspectives that can guide content refinement. An open dialogue with viewers enables creators to identify what resonates, what requires adjustment, and what fresh ideas can be woven into future content.

Community Building: A Shared Sense of Belonging

The heart of audience interaction is community building. When viewers feel heard and valued, they develop a sense of belonging. This shared affinity encourages viewers to return, engage in discussions, and even develop connections with fellow audience members. A strong community can extend beyond the YouTube platform, with dedicated fans forming bonds that enrich both their own experiences and the creator's journey.

Humanizing the Creator: Relatability and Authenticity

Interaction humanizes creators, bridging the gap between the person on-screen and the viewers behind the screens. Sharing personal anecdotes, responding to questions, and even addressing challenges you've faced can create a relatable persona. This authenticity resonates with viewers, engendering trust and encouraging them to invest emotionally in your content.

Incorporating Viewer Suggestions: A Collaborative Approach

Incorporating viewer suggestions is the embodiment of a collaborative creator-viewer relationship. When you listen to your audience's ideas, you demonstrate respect for their creative input. These suggestions can inspire new content ideas, inform direction, or even result in collaborative projects that give viewers a sense of ownership over the channel's growth.

Time Management and Consistency

While engaging with viewers is paramount, effective time management is key. Dedicate specific times for interacting with comments and engaging on social media to ensure a consistent presence. While it may be challenging to respond to every comment, acknowledging a representative sample showcases your commitment to interaction.

Navigating Constructive Criticism

Not all feedback will be positive, but embracing constructive criticism is an opportunity for growth. Responding professionally and courteously to criticism showcases your openness to diverse perspectives. It's a chance to demonstrate maturity and learn from your audience's viewpoints.

Creating a Positive Feedback Loop

Audience interaction creates a feedback loop that enriches content creation. Comments and feedback offer insights, while your responses demonstrate active listening. As content evolves based on viewer input, viewers feel a sense of contribution, reinforcing their commitment to your channel.

Impact Beyond Metrics: A Legacy of Connection

In conclusion, audience interaction transcends numerical metrics; it's about building genuine connections that transcend the digital realm. By responding to comments, seeking feedback, and incorporating viewer suggestions, you lay the foundation for a vibrant community that rallies around your content. Your viewers transform into participants, and your channel evolves into a platform for meaningful discourse and shared experiences. As you navigate the path of audience interaction, remember that the legacy you're creating extends beyond the likes and views – it's about nurturing relationships, sparking conversations, and leaving an enduring imprint on the intricate tapestry of YouTube.

8 Social Media Promotion: Utilize various social media platforms to promote your videos and engage with a wider audience.

Unleashing the Power of Social Media: Elevating Your YouTube Presence Through Strategic Promotion

In the dynamic landscape of YouTube content creation, the strategic utilization of social media platforms emerges as a pivotal strategy for creators seeking to extend their reach, foster engagement, and cultivate a thriving online community. This deliberate practice involves leveraging the diverse avenues offered by social media to promote your videos, connect with audiences beyond YouTube, and amplify your content's impact. By harnessing the potential of social media promotion, you not only elevate your video's discoverability but also forge meaningful connections that transcend the confines of the YouTube screen.

Unveiling the Essence of Social Media Promotion

Social media promotion is a multifaceted tool that empowers creators to reach audiences beyond their YouTube subscriber base. It involves using various social platforms, such as Twitter, Instagram, Facebook, and TikTok, to amplify your content's visibility, initiate discussions, and engage with viewers on a broader scale. By strategically promoting your videos on social media, you tap into a wider audience pool and create a holistic digital presence.

Expanding Reach: Tapping into Diverse Audiences

Each social media platform boasts a unique user base, demographics, and communication style. By extending your content's reach to these platforms, you tap into previously untapped audiences who might resonate with your content. From short-form video platforms like TikTok to visual-centric platforms like Instagram, your content can find its niche across diverse online ecosystems.

Content Teasers: Piquing Curiosity

Social media acts as a gateway to your YouTube content. Posting teaser content – such as short video snippets, captivating images, or intriguing captions – generates anticipation for your videos. These teasers pique curiosity and prompt viewers to venture onto your YouTube channel to consume the full content, thereby driving up engagement and watch time.

Engagement Boost: Fostering Conversations

Social media isn't just a promotional megaphone; it's a dialogue facilitator. Engage with your audience by responding to comments, asking questions, and soliciting opinions. These interactions foster a sense of connection and encourage audiences to delve into your YouTube content, where they can participate in more in-depth discussions.

Strategic Timing: Maximizing Visibility

Posting your content on social media requires a strategic approach to timing. Consider the peak activity times of your target audience on each platform. Utilize scheduling tools to ensure your posts are visible when your audience is most active. This strategic timing enhances the likelihood of your content gaining traction and being seen by a larger audience.

Platform Synergy: Tailoring Content for Each Platform

While cross-promoting is effective, it's crucial to tailor your content to suit the nuances of each platform. Twitter demands concise messaging, Instagram thrives on visual appeal, and TikTok calls for snappy videos. Adapting your content for each platform ensures it aligns with the platform's style and resonates with its audience.

Hashtags and Trends: Riding the Digital Currents

Hashtags and trends act as conduits to digital conversations. Utilize relevant hashtags to amplify your content's visibility within trending topics. Engaging with trending discussions showcases your relevance and might draw users to explore your content, thereby expanding your audience.

Collaborations and Partnerships: Amplifying Reach

Social media platforms are fertile ground for collaborations and partnerships. Co-create content with fellow creators, participate in challenges, or collaborate on live streams. These ventures introduce your channel to new audiences and enrich your content through diverse perspectives.

Community Building: Fostering Loyalty

Social media acts as an extension of your YouTube community. By engaging consistently and authentically, you foster a loyal following that transcends platforms. Responding to comments, sharing behind-the-scenes glimpses, and even involving your audience in content decisions create a sense of belonging that strengthens viewer loyalty.

Analyzing Insights: Informed Decision-Making

Most social media platforms offer analytics tools that provide insights into post engagement, audience demographics, and more. These insights inform your promotion strategies, helping you refine your approach and focus on platforms and content styles that resonate most effectively with your audience.

Legacy of Connection: Building a Digital Universe

In conclusion, social media promotion is a strategic lever that extends your content's impact far beyond the confines of YouTube. By harnessing the unique strengths of different platforms, you create a digital universe where your content thrives and conversations flourish. Your strategic promotion efforts foster connections, spark discussions, and cultivate a loyal community that spans multiple platforms. As you navigate the realm of social media promotion, remember that each post, comment, and interaction contributes to a legacy of engagement, interaction, and influence in the dynamic tapestry of online content creation.

9 Collaborations: Collaborate with fellow YouTubers to cross-promote and tap into their audiences.

The Art of Collaborative Creation: Elevating Your YouTube Presence Through Strategic Collaborations

In the ever-evolving realm of YouTube content creation, the power of collaborations stands as a transformative strategy for creators aiming to extend their reach, amplify engagement, and forge lasting partnerships within the digital landscape. This purposeful practice involves teaming up with fellow YouTubers to create content that leverages each other's strengths, cross-promotes, and taps into diverse audiences. By embracing the potential of collaborations, you not only enhance your content's visibility but also cultivate a dynamic network that resonates with viewers and enriches the creative journey.

Unveiling the Essence of Collaborations

Collaborations on YouTube are more than shared screen time; they're synergistic alliances that blend individual creativity to produce engaging, multifaceted content. Whether it's co-hosting a video, participating in a challenge, or crafting joint narratives, collaborations tap into the collective strengths of creators to deliver enriched experiences to audiences.

Expanded Reach: Bridging Audiences

The true magic of collaborations lies in the expansion of reach. By partnering with creators from different niches, you gain access to their dedicated audiences. This cross-pollination introduces your content to viewers who might not have discovered your channel otherwise. This increased exposure not only boosts views but also cultivates new subscribers and fosters a sense of community beyond your established base.

Fusion of Creativity: Unique Perspectives

Collaborations infuse content with fresh perspectives. The amalgamation of diverse voices, styles, and ideas creates a dynamic blend that captivates viewers. Collaborators bring their unique creative flair, enriching the narrative and offering a novel experience that resonates with audiences across both channels.

Strategic Synergy: Choosing Collaborators

Collaboration partners should align with your content's ethos and resonate with your audience. Seek creators whose values, interests, and style complement yours. An effective collaboration should feel genuine and not forced. This strategic synergy ensures that the partnership benefits both parties authentically.

Complementary Skills: Crafting Enriched Content

Effective collaborations capitalize on complementary skills. If you're adept at storytelling, partner with a creator skilled in visual effects. By combining expertise, you elevate the quality of your content, offering viewers a holistic experience that caters to their diverse preferences.

Audience Engagement: Fostering Enthusiasm

Collaborations invigorate viewer enthusiasm. Audiences are drawn to the anticipation of seeing their favorite creators team up. This excitement fuels engagement, driving up views, likes, and comments. Collaborations generate buzz and discussions that extend beyond the videos themselves.

Cross-Promotion: Mutual Benefit

Collaborations facilitate mutual cross-promotion. By featuring each other's channels in videos and leveraging social media platforms, you introduce your partner's audience to your content and vice versa. This strategic exchange reinforces the sense of community and encourages audiences to explore both channels.

Incorporating Different Styles: Expanding Horizons

Collaborations encourage creators to step out of their comfort zones. Exploring different content styles, tones, or genres broadens horizons and introduces your audience to varied forms of entertainment. This experimentation keeps your content fresh and bolsters viewer engagement.

Community Building: Forming Bonds

Collaborations forge bonds not only between creators but also between audiences. Shared experiences create a sense of camaraderie that unites viewers across channels. Audiences connect over mutual appreciation for the collaborative content, further enriching the sense of community.

Creative Learning: Skill Exchange

Collaborations offer a platform for creators to learn from each other. Exchange of techniques, strategies, and creative processes enhances skills and cultivates growth. This mutual learning benefits both creators and, ultimately, the audience that benefits from enriched content.

Long-Term Partnerships: Nurturing Relationships

Collaborations have the potential to evolve into long-term partnerships. When you find creators who resonate with your vision, the collaboration can extend beyond a single video. These relationships deepen, leading to more engaging and impactful content for both audiences.

Impact Beyond Videos: A Tapestry of Connection
In conclusion, collaborations transcend mere videos; they weave a tapestry of connection that resonates with audiences and enriches content creation. By leveraging the strengths of fellow YouTubers, you expand your reach, amplify engagement, and foster dynamic community growth. Collaborations embody the ethos of shared creativity and mutual support, nurturing relationships that extend beyond the digital realm. As you navigate the realm of collaborative creation, remember that every partnership you forge, every idea you coalesce, and every shared experience you create contribute to a legacy of camaraderie, exploration, and impact in the ever-evolving landscape of YouTube.

10 Analytics Insight: Regularly analyze your video performance using analytics tools to refine your strategy based on viewer trends

The Art of Data Mastery: Elevating Your YouTube Strategy Through Informed Insights
In the dynamic realm of YouTube content creation, the mastery of analytics insight stands as a pivotal strategy for creators aiming to refine their approach, amplify engagement, and align their content with viewer preferences. This deliberate practice involves harnessing the power of analytics tools to dissect video performance, unravel viewer trends, and make data-driven decisions that optimize content delivery. By embracing the potential of analytics insight, you not only enhance your content's resonance but also cultivate a deeper understanding of your audience's desires, aspirations, and engagement patterns.

Unveiling the Essence of Analytics Insight
Analytics insight offers creators a window into the minds of their audience. It's a treasure trove of data that encompasses a video's performance metrics, viewer demographics, engagement patterns, and more. By extracting meaningful insights from this data, creators gain the ability to tailor their content strategy,

refine their storytelling, and curate experiences that resonate more powerfully with their viewers.

Viewer Behaviour: Unraveling Engagement Patterns

Analytics tools provide a detailed view of viewer behaviour. You can discern when viewers drop off, where they engage most, and even the specific points where they rewind or replay sections. This granular understanding allows you to identify engagement hotspots and optimize your content to maintain viewer interest throughout the video.

Content Evaluation: Refining Quality

Analyzing viewer metrics offers a critical evaluation of your content's quality. High retention rates indicate captivating storytelling, while low retention rates might signify areas that need improvement. Insights into average watch time help you discern which types of content resonate most effectively with your audience, guiding your future content creation efforts.

Demographics and Geolocation: Tailoring Content

Analytics unveil the demographics and geolocation of your audience. This insight is a golden key to tailoring content that aligns with your viewer's interests, values, and cultural nuances. By understanding who your audience is, you can create content that transcends borders and resonates on a personal level.

Keyword Performance: Enhancing Discoverability

Analytics tools offer insights into the search terms that lead viewers to your content. Understanding the keywords that are driving traffic to your videos allows you to refine your content's title, description, and tags. This optimization enhances your video's discoverability and boosts its visibility in search results.

Audience Retention: Crafting Engaging Content

Audience retention metrics reveal the effectiveness of your content in keeping viewers engaged. By analyzing when viewers tend to drop off, you can identify potential pain points or areas that might require more captivating visuals, pacing adjustments, or concise storytelling.

Click-Through Rate: Crafting Compelling Thumbnails and Titles

The click-through rate (CTR) is a powerful indicator of the effectiveness of your thumbnails and titles. A low CTR suggests that your thumbnails and titles might not be resonating with potential viewers. By analyzing CTR trends, you can refine your visual and textual elements to create compelling and enticing thumbnails that capture clicks.

Mobile vs. Desktop Engagement: Adaptive Strategy

Understanding the platforms through which viewers access your content is pivotal. Analyzing the engagement patterns between mobile and desktop users guides you in creating content that suits different viewing environments. This adaptive strategy ensures that your content is accessible and engaging regardless of the device.

Time of Day and Posting Frequency: Strategic Scheduling

Analytics tools reveal when your audience is most active. Posting your content during these peak times enhances its visibility and engagement. Additionally, analyzing the performance of different posting frequencies helps you determine the optimal cadence that keeps your audience consistently engaged.

Iterative Improvement: Refining the Approach

Regularly analyzing your video performance instills a culture of continuous improvement. Analyze how changes in strategy impact metrics, and adapt accordingly. Whether it's experimenting with content formats, refining thumbnail designs, or adjusting posting times, this iterative approach helps you refine your content creation process based on informed insights.

Long-Term Strategy: Viewer Trends

Tracking viewer trends over time uncovers overarching patterns that shape your content strategy. By identifying consistent engagement peaks, preferred content formats, and emerging viewer preferences, you can tailor your long-term strategy to maintain viewer interest and engagement.

Impact Beyond Metrics: Creating Meaningful Connections

In conclusion, analytics insight transcends numerical metrics; it's about creating meaningful connections between creators and audiences. By delving into the data, you unlock the secrets to viewer engagement, preferences, and aspirations. These insights guide your content strategy, fostering resonance, trust, and loyalty. As you navigate the realm of analytics insight, remember that each data point is a window into the hearts and minds of your viewers, and your ability to harness this data contributes to a legacy of content that captivates, empowers, and leaves an indelible mark on the dynamic canvas of YouTube.

11 Mobile-Friendly Content: Ensure your videos are optimized for mobile viewing, as a significant portion of YouTube traffic comes from mobile devices.

Crafting Mobile Marvels: Optimizing YouTube Content for Seamless Mobile Viewing

In the vibrant realm of YouTube content creation, the mastery of mobile-friendly content stands as a pivotal strategy for creators aiming to captivate audiences, amplify engagement, and cater to the evolving preferences of modern viewers. This intentional approach involves tailoring video content to ensure optimal viewing experiences on mobile devices, acknowledging the significant portion of YouTube traffic that originates from smartphones and tablets. By embracing the potential of mobile-friendly content, creators not only enhance their content's accessibility but also tap into a dynamic avenue for connection, interaction, and lasting impact.

Unveiling the Essence of Mobile-Friendly Content

Mobile-friendly content is more than just adapting to smaller screens; it's about crafting experiences that resonate powerfully with mobile viewers. With a substantial chunk of YouTube traffic flowing from mobile devices, creating content that's easily consumable, visually engaging, and seamlessly navigable on small screens is paramount.

Responsive Design: Adapting to Variable Screens

Responsive design is the cornerstone of mobile-friendly content. Ensure that your videos adapt fluidly to various screen sizes and orientations. This design approach guarantees that your content remains engaging, regardless of whether it's viewed on a smartphone, tablet, or desktop monitor.

Vertical Video: Capitalizing on Mobile Orientation

The rise of vertical video is closely tied to mobile viewing habits. Shooting or formatting content in a vertical orientation maximizes screen real estate, offering an immersive viewing experience that aligns with how mobile users naturally hold their devices. Embracing vertical video not only accommodates mobile viewers but also provides a fresh creative canvas for storytelling.

Captivating Thumbnails and Titles: Mobile-Optimized Appeal
Thumbnails and titles play a crucial role in mobile discovery.
With limited screen space, it's essential to craft visually
captivating thumbnails that entice viewers to click. Similarly,
titles should be concise yet compelling, conveying the essence of
the content in a glance.

Brief Introductions: Grabbing Attention Quickly
Mobile viewers have shorter attention spans, making concise
introductions essential. Capture viewers' interest within the first
few seconds to prevent them from scrolling past your video. A
gripping hook or a sneak peek at the main content can be highly
effective in retaining mobile viewers' attention.

Clear Visuals and Text: Enhancing Readability
Mobile screens are smaller, which can lead to challenges in
visual clarity. Ensure that text, graphics, and visuals are easily
legible on mobile devices. Using larger fonts, high-contrast
colours, and clear visual elements enhances readability and
ensures that your content is comprehensible even on smaller
screens.

Engaging Thumbnails: Mobile-Centric Design
Thumbnails should be designed with mobile consumption in
mind. Test your thumbnails on different mobile devices to ensure
that they're eye-catching and effectively convey the video's
essence, even at smaller sizes.

Narrative Flow: Mobile-Compatible Structure
Consider the pacing and structure of your videos with mobile
viewers in mind. Break content into digestible segments, use
concise storytelling techniques, and avoid lengthy tangents. A
streamlined narrative flow ensures that mobile viewers remain
engaged throughout the video.

Closed Captions: Ensuring Accessibility
Closed captions enhance the accessibility of your content,
catering to viewers who watch without sound or those who may
have hearing impairments. Captions are especially beneficial on
mobile devices where viewers might be in public spaces or
environments where audio isn't feasible.

Vertical Navigation: Intuitive User Experience
Ensure that your video's navigation and controls are optimized
for vertical viewing. Mobile users interact with their devices in a

different manner than desktop users, so placing essential navigation elements within easy reach enhances the user experience.

Loading Speed: Swift Access to Content

Mobile viewers value speed. Ensure that your videos load quickly to prevent viewers from losing interest due to slow loading times. Compressing videos and optimizing image sizes can significantly enhance loading speed.

Viewability: Crafting for Smaller Screens

Design your video content with smaller screens in mind. Avoid intricate visual details that might be lost on mobile devices and opt for bold, simple visuals that remain impactful even on diminutive screens.

Impact Beyond Boundaries: Crafting Connections

In conclusion, mobile-friendly content creation is a testament to the adaptability and innovation inherent in the YouTube landscape. By optimizing videos for mobile viewing, creators extend their reach to a vast mobile audience while delivering captivating experiences that resonate powerfully. Mobile-friendly content isn't just about screen dimensions; it's about crafting connections that transcend devices and foster engagement, interaction, and resonance. As you navigate the realm of mobile-friendly content, remember that each optimized element contributes to a legacy of seamless experiences, resonant storytelling, and meaningful connections in the ever-evolving canvas of YouTube.

12 Compelling Introductions: Hook viewers from the start with engaging introductions that highlight the value of your content.

Captivating Entrances: Crafting Engaging Introductions to Hook Viewers from the Start

In the dynamic world of YouTube content creation, the mastery of compelling introductions stands as a pivotal strategy for creators aiming to captivate audiences, amplify engagement, and entice viewers to delve deeper into their content. This deliberate practice involves crafting opening sequences that grab viewers' attention, highlight the value of the content, and establish an immediate connection. By harnessing the potential of compelling introductions, creators not only enhance their video's watch time but also create a strong foundation for a viewer's journey through the content, ensuring that they stay engaged and invested until the very end.

Unveiling the Essence of Compelling Introductions

A compelling introduction is more than just a preliminary segment; it's the hook that draws viewers into the narrative. This is the moment where creators have the opportunity to make a powerful first impression, set the tone for the content, and showcase the value viewers can expect to gain from watching.

The First Impression: Crafting a Powerful Hook

First impressions are lasting, and an engaging introduction is your chance to make an impact. Whether it's through a thought-provoking question, a tantalizing teaser, or an intriguing anecdote, the opening moments should compel viewers to pause, watch, and explore further.

Value Proposition: Showcasing Content Benefits

The introduction should convey the value of the content to viewers. What will they gain from investing their time? Whether it's entertainment, information, inspiration, or practical advice, the introduction should offer a glimpse of the benefits that await them.

Emotional Resonance: Stirring Viewer Connection

Emotion is the cornerstone of engagement. A compelling introduction taps into viewers' emotions, evoking curiosity, excitement, surprise, or empathy. By creating an emotional resonance, you establish a connection that keeps viewers invested in the journey.

Establishing Context: Setting the Scene

Context is crucial for viewer comprehension. The introduction should establish the framework of the content – what the video aims to address, explore, or resolve. Providing context helps viewers understand the relevance and significance of the content to their interests or concerns.

Storytelling: Weaving Intriguing Narratives

Humans are wired for stories, and a well-crafted narrative can be a compelling introduction. Whether it's sharing a personal experience, presenting a relatable scenario, or unveiling a mystery, storytelling draws viewers in, creating a sense of anticipation for what's to come.

Visual Engagement: Using Visual Elements
Visual appeal is a potent tool in introductions. Utilize captivating visuals, animations, or compelling shots that hint at the content's themes. Visual intrigue not only grabs attention but also adds an extra layer of engagement.

Surprising Elements: Sparking Curiosity
Introductions can leverage surprise to pique curiosity. Teasing a surprising fact, revealing an unexpected twist, or presenting a provocative statement sparks curiosity and prompts viewers to continue watching to uncover the full story.

Concise Delivery: Keeping it Snappy
In the fast-paced digital world, brevity is key. Keep your introduction concise while packing it with intrigue. A succinct, impactful introduction ensures that viewers' attention is captured before it starts to waver.

Call to Action: Encouraging Engagement
A well-placed call to action can be integrated into the introduction. Encourage viewers to like, subscribe, or leave a comment. This early engagement not only establishes a sense of interactivity but also primes viewers for further interaction.

Voice and Tone: Reflecting the Content
The introduction sets the tone for the entire video. Align the voice, tone, and style of your introduction with the content's overall message. Whether it's light-hearted, informative, or thought-provoking, the introduction should provide a glimpse of what viewers can expect.

Testing and Iteration: Enhancing Impact
Creating compelling introductions is an iterative process. Test different approaches and analyze viewer engagement metrics to understand what resonates most effectively with your audience. Continuously refine your introduction strategy based on data-driven insights.

Sustaining Engagement: A Launch Pad for Success
In conclusion, a compelling introduction is more than just a threshold; it's a launch pad for viewer engagement and content resonance. By crafting introductions that captivate, showcase value, and establish a connection, creators set the stage for a viewer's immersive experience. These initial moments shape the trajectory of viewer engagement, ensuring that audiences stay

invested, watch longer, and connect more deeply with the content. As you navigate the art of compelling introductions, remember that each captivating opening is an invitation to explore, discover, and forge connections in the dynamic tapestry of YouTube content creation.

13 Storyboarding: Plan your videos with clear storyboards to maintain a coherent structure and narrative flow.

Visualizing Excellence: Elevating YouTube Videos Through Effective Storyboarding

In the captivating realm of YouTube content creation, the art of storyboarding stands as a pivotal strategy for creators aiming to craft seamless videos, maintain narrative coherence, and guide viewers on a compelling journey. This deliberate practice involves the meticulous planning of videos through visual storyboards, which outline the structure, flow, and visual elements of the content. By embracing the potential of storyboarding, creators not only enhance the storytelling quality of their videos but also ensure that every frame aligns with the intended message, creating a rich and immersive viewer experience.

Unveiling the Essence of Storyboarding

Storyboarding is more than a mere preparatory step; it's the blueprint that shapes the video's entire narrative. It involves breaking down the content into visual sequences, ensuring that each frame flows seamlessly into the next. Storyboarding empowers creators to visualize their ideas, refine the structure, and create content that engages viewers from start to finish.

Visualizing the Narrative: Structured Framework

Storyboards provide a visual framework for the narrative. This enables creators to organize their content into coherent segments, ensuring a logical progression of ideas and events. With a structured framework in place, creators can avoid tangents, maintain focus, and deliver a clear and impactful message.

Scene-by-Scene Flow: Crafting Cohesiveness

Each scene in a video contributes to the overall narrative flow. Storyboarding breaks down the video into individual shots, allowing creators to see how each scene connects with the next. This holistic view ensures that scenes transition seamlessly, maintaining viewer engagement and preventing disjointed storytelling.

Visual Elements: Precise Composition

Storyboarding isn't limited to plot; it also involves planning visual elements. Creators can outline camera angles, compositions, and shot types, ensuring that the visual presentation enhances the storytelling. This meticulous planning results in a visually captivating and cohesive video.

Pacing and Timing: Guiding Audience Experience

Storyboarding facilitates control over pacing and timing. Creators can determine how long each scene will last, ensuring that the video's rhythm aligns with the narrative's emotional beats. This strategic control over pacing enhances viewer engagement and emotional resonance.

Visual Engagement: Crafting Impactful Shots

Effective shots are pivotal in video storytelling. Storyboards help creators visualize how each shot contributes to the narrative's impact. By planning engaging visuals, creators create a dynamic viewing experience that captures attention and sustains engagement.

Storyboard Consistency: Ensuring Alignment

Storyboarding maintains consistency throughout the video. It ensures that visual elements, character positions, and scene continuity remain aligned from one shot to the next. This meticulous attention to detail eliminates inconsistencies that could disrupt the viewer's immersion.

Guiding Creativity: Creative Direction

Storyboarding offers a canvas for creative exploration. Creators can experiment with different compositions, camera movements, and visual effects on paper before filming. This enables the visualization of creative ideas and ensures that the final video aligns with the intended vision.

Collaboration Facilitation: Unified Vision

In collaborative projects, storyboards foster a unified vision among team members. Whether it's a scriptwriter, director, or cinematographer, a clear storyboard ensures that everyone is on the same page, contributing to a harmonious and efficient production process.

Flexibility and Iteration: Enhancing Quality

Storyboarding allows for creative flexibility and iterative improvement. Creators can review the storyboard and identify areas for enhancement before production begins. This iterative process ensures that the video's structure, visuals, and narrative elements align seamlessly.

Coherent Narratives: A Journey of Excellence

In conclusion, storyboarding transcends being a mere prelude to video creation; it's a transformative tool that shapes coherent narratives, guides creative direction, and crafts captivating visual journeys. By visualizing the video's structure, flow, and visual elements, creators ensure that their content resonates powerfully with viewers. Storyboarding empowers creators to bring their ideas to life while maintaining a seamless narrative flow that captivates, informs, and entertains. As you navigate the realm of storyboarding, remember that each frame you meticulously plan contributes to a legacy of storytelling excellence, creating connections, and leaving a lasting imprint on the dynamic canvas of YouTube content creation.

14 Personal Branding: Develop a strong and relatable personal brand that resonates with your target audience.

Crafting Authenticity: The Power of Personal Branding for YouTube Creators

In the ever-evolving landscape of YouTube content creation, the art of personal branding stands as a pivotal strategy for creators aiming to establish an authentic identity, forge deeper connections with their audience, and leave an indelible mark on the digital realm. This intentional practice involves developing a unique and relatable personal brand that resonates with the target audience's values, aspirations, and interests. By embracing the potential of personal branding, creators not only enhance their content's impact but also build a lasting legacy founded on authenticity, resonance, and meaningful connections.

Unveiling the Essence of Personal Branding

Personal branding transcends the superficial; it's the embodiment of a creator's values, persona, and the unique blend that makes them relatable and memorable. It's about shaping an identity that resonates authentically with the audience, forging an emotional connection that transcends the screen.

Distinctive Identity: Unveiling Your Essence

At the core of personal branding is a distinctive identity. Creators must define who they are, what they stand for, and how they're different from others in the field. This distinctiveness not only sets creators apart but also forms the foundation of their personal brand.

Audience Alignment: Meeting Viewer Desires

Personal branding doesn't just serve the creator; it serves the audience. Creators must align their personal brand with their target audience's desires, values, and preferences. Understanding your audience's needs enables you to craft content that genuinely resonates.

Authenticity: A Foundation of Trust

Authenticity is the bedrock of personal branding. Creators must be true to themselves, showcasing their real selves rather than a fabricated persona. Authenticity fosters trust, creating a genuine connection that viewers appreciate and identify with.

Consistency: Building Recognition

Consistency reinforces personal branding. From content style and visual aesthetics to communication tone, a consistent approach creates recognizability. Viewers should be able to identify a creator's content simply by its distinct qualities.

Relatability: Nurturing Emotional Connection

Personal branding involves becoming relatable to your audience. Creators should share personal experiences, struggles, and triumphs that viewers can identify with. This vulnerability creates an emotional connection that fosters viewer loyalty.

Storytelling: Weaving a Narrative Thread

Storytelling is a potent tool for personal branding. Creators can weave their personal journey into their content, sharing anecdotes that illustrate their values and growth. These narratives engage viewers and create an authentic connection.

Visual Identity: Reflecting Personality

Visual elements play a role in personal branding. Creators should cultivate a visual style – from logos to thumbnails – that reflects their personality and resonates with their audience. Visual consistency reinforces the brand's identity.

Engagement and Interaction: Active Connection

Interaction is a cornerstone of personal branding. Creators should engage with their audience through comments, social media, and community engagement. This two-way communication strengthens the connection and demonstrates a genuine interest in viewer perspectives.

Value Proposition: Offering Unique Benefits

Personal branding extends to the value creators provide. By defining what unique benefits viewers gain from their content, creators solidify their personal brand's promise and purpose. This ensures that their content consistently aligns with viewer expectations.

Feedback Incorporation: Adapting and Growing

Personal branding is a dynamic process. Creators should be open to feedback, adapting and growing based on audience input. This responsiveness not only enhances personal branding but also showcases the creator's commitment to improvement.

Legacy of Resonance: A Mark of Influence

In conclusion, personal branding isn't a mere badge; it's a legacy of resonance, authenticity, and influence. By shaping a distinctive identity that aligns with their audience's values, creators create a connection that goes beyond views and likes. Personal branding is about leaving an indelible mark on the digital landscape – a mark that's rooted in authenticity, defined by shared values, and enriched by meaningful interactions. As you navigate the realm of personal branding, remember that your authenticity is your greatest asset, and the personal brand you cultivate leaves an enduring imprint on the vibrant tapestry of YouTube content creation.

15 Patience and Persistence: Building a successful YouTube channel takes tim e. Stay patient, adapt to changes, and persistently refine your approach.

Nurturing Success: The Virtues of Patience and Persistence in YouTube Journey

In the dynamic universe of YouTube content creation, the virtues of patience and persistence stand as the guiding lights for creators aiming to carve a path of success, adapt to evolving landscapes, and craft a legacy of meaningful impact. This enduring practice involves acknowledging that building a successful YouTube channel is a journey that demands time, resilience, and a willingness to evolve. By embracing the potential of patience and persistence, creators not only fortify their resilience but also ensure that their journey is a testament to growth, adaptability, and the power of unwavering dedication.

Unveiling the Essence of Patience and Persistence

Patience and persistence are more than just clichés; they're the cornerstones of a sustainable and thriving YouTube journey. These virtues remind creators that success is rarely instantaneous – it's a culmination of steady effort, continuous learning, and the willingness to navigate challenges with determination.

Time as a Valuable Asset: Embracing the Journey

Patience requires understanding that building a successful YouTube channel takes time. Rather than seeking immediate gratification, creators should focus on nurturing their content, engaging with their audience, and steadily progressing towards their goals. The journey itself becomes an enriching experience, fostering growth and maturation.

Adaptability to Changes: Embracing Evolution

Persistence involves an unwavering commitment to adaptability. The digital landscape is ever-changing, with algorithms, trends, and viewer preferences constantly evolving. Creators who persistently adjust their strategies to align with these changes remain relevant and resilient in a dynamic environment.

The Power of Learning: Continuous Improvement

Patience and persistence nurture a culture of continuous learning. Creators should be open to feedback, analyze their performance, and seek ways to refine their content and strategy. Each setback becomes a learning opportunity, contributing to improved content quality and strategy effectiveness.

Overcoming Challenges: Strengthening Resilience

Persistence shines brightest in the face of challenges. Whether it's facing algorithm shifts, content fluctuations, or viewer engagement hurdles, creators who persistently seek solutions, innovate, and overcome obstacles build a strong foundation of resilience that sustains their journey.

Quality over Quantity: Fostering Excellence

Patience and persistence underscore the importance of quality over quantity. While growth may be gradual, it's the commitment to delivering valuable, well-crafted content that builds viewer trust and loyalty. Creators who prioritize quality content are more likely to achieve enduring success.

Audience Building: Gradual Connection

Building an audience is a gradual process. Creators should nurture their community, engage with their viewers, and foster a sense of belonging. Over time, this connection deepens, resulting in a dedicated audience that becomes a driving force for channel growth.

Iterative Refinement: Evolving Strategies

Both patience and persistence advocate for an iterative approach. Creators should regularly assess their strategies, seek data-driven insights, and refine their approach accordingly. This adapt-and-refine cycle ensures that their content remains relevant and resonant.

Long-Term Vision: Building Legacies

Patience and persistence encourage creators to adopt a long-term vision. Rather than focusing solely on short-term metrics, they should envision the lasting impact they can make through consistent, value-driven content. This forward-looking perspective sustains motivation and guides decision-making.

Celebrating Milestones: Honouring Progress

Amid the journey's challenges, celebrating milestones is essential. Creators should acknowledge and cherish the growth, achievements, and milestones they reach. These moments of celebration reinforce the progress made and offer renewed energy for the path ahead.

A Journey of Inspiration: Leaving a Mark

In conclusion, the virtues of patience and persistence transform a YouTube journey into a saga of inspiration, growth, and meaningful impact. By embracing the value of time, adaptability, and unwavering commitment, creators build a legacy that resonates beyond numbers and statistics. Patience and persistence aren't just means to an end; they're the heart and soul of a journey that's defined by overcoming obstacles, adapting to change, and crafting content that leaves a lasting imprint on the ever-evolving tapestry of YouTube content creation. As you navigate the path of patience and persistence, remember that every step you take, every challenge you overcome, and every improvement you make contributes to a legacy that reflects the spirit of resilience and the pursuit of excellence.

Conclusion:

In the captivating realm of YouTube, success is an evolving masterpiece, woven through passion, persistence, and purpose. Crafting a successful channel requires embracing niche expertise, captivating content, SEO prowess, and unwavering audience engagement. It thrives on authenticity, strategic collaborations, and an adaptive approach to evolving trends. From compelling introductions to mobile-friendly mastery, every aspect is meticulously woven into a tapestry of excellence. With each creation, connection, and milestone, a legacy of influence is etched onto the digital canvas. Remember, the journey is a fusion of dedication and creativity, where success is not just a destination, but a dynamic masterpiece in constant evolution.

The ENd

www.ingramcontent.com/pod-product-compliance
Lightning Source LLC
LaVergne TN
LVHW010041070326
832903LV00071B/4746